# LEIF *Eriksson*

SPIRIT
of America®

LEIF *Eriksson*

NORWEGIAN EXPLORER

*By Cynthia Klingel and Robert B. Noyed*

The
Child's
World

*The Child's World®*
*Chanhassen, Minnesota*

8

# Leif *Eriksson*

*Published in the United States of America by The Child's World®*
PO Box 326 • Chanhassen, MN 55317-0326 • 800-599-READ • www.childsworld.com

*Acknowledgments*
The Child's World®: Mary Berendes, Publishing Director

Editorial Directions, Inc.: E. Russell Primm, Emily Dolbear, and Lucia Raatma, Editors; Linda S. Koutris, Photo Selector; Dawn Friedman, Photo Research; Red Line Editorial, Fact Research; Irene Keller, Copy Editor; Tim Griffin/IndexServ, Indexer; Chad Rubel, Proofreader

*Photos*
Cover: Library of Congress, Washington, DC/Bridgeman Art Library; National Museum, Copenhagen, Denmark/Werner Forman/Art Resource, NY: 9, 17; Formist Museum, Denmark/D.Y./Art Resource, NY: 14; Werner Forman/Art Resource, NY: 15 top; Viking Ship Museum, Bygdoy, Norway/Werner Forman/Art Resource, NY: 20; Monastery of La Rabida, Palos de la Frontera, Spain/Giraudon/Art Resource, NY: 26 bottom; Library of Congress, Washington, DC/Bridgeman Art Library: 2; Nasjonalgalleriet, Oslo, Norway/Bridgeman Art Library: 21 top; Chris Lisle/Corbis: 6; Bettmann/Corbis: 7 top, 8, 19; Paul Almasy/Corbis: 7 bottom; Wolfgang Kaehler/Corbis: 11, 12; W. Perry Conway/Corbis: 15 bottom; Galen Rowell/Corbis: 21 bottom; Colin Braley/Reuters NewMedia Inc./Corbis: 23; James Davis; Eye Ubiquitous/Corbis: 28; Hulton Archive/Getty Images: 16; North Wind Picture Archives: 13, 25, 27; Stock Montage: 22, 26 top.

*Registration*
The Child's World®, Spirit of America®, and their associated logos are the sole property and registered trademarks of The Child's World®.

*Library of Congress Cataloging-in-Publication Data*
Klingel, Cynthia Fitterer.
Leif Eriksson : Norwegian explorer / by Cynthia Klingel and Robert B. Noyed.
        p. cm. — (Spirit of America)
Summary: A brief introduction to the life and accomplishments of the
Norwegian explorer Leif Eriksson.
ISBN 1-56766-163-7 (Library Bound : alk. paper)
1. Leiv Eiriksson, d. ca. 1020—Juvenile literature. 2. Explorers—America—Biography—Juvenile literature.
3. Explorers—Norway—Biography—Juvenile literature. 4. America—Discovery and exploration—Norse—Juvenile
literature. 5. Vikings—Juvenile literature. [1. Ericson, Leif, d. ca. 1020. 2. Explorers. 3. Vikings.
4. America—Discovery and exploration—Norse.] I. Noyed, Robert B. II. Title. III. Series.
E105.L47 K58 2002
970.01'3'092—dc21

2001007818

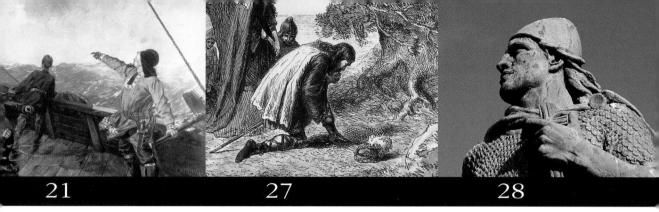

21    27    28

# Contents

## Chapter ONE

# Son of Erik the Red

*Today, most Norwegians live by the sea as they did in the days of the Vikings.*

LONG BEFORE CHRISTOPHER COLUMBUS CAME to North America in 1492, Norwegian explorers had discovered this new land. Leif Eriksson led these explorers. He was a sailor from the country now known as Norway. The events in this book took place more than 1,000 years ago.

Long ago, the **Vikings** ruled Norway. The Vikings were fierce pirates and warriors who sailed in the icy waters of the North Sea. They

6

explored its waters looking for new lands to conquer.

The Vikings made many trips to explore and conquer new land.

Iceland is a large island west of Norway. Although its name suggests that it is a cold place, Iceland is really a pleasant place to live. The warm sea currents keep Iceland from getting too cold. And fish are plentiful in the oceans around the island.

*Fishing boats dock at the port of Heimaey in Iceland. Vikings also fished in these waters.*

Thousands of Viking people left Norway to settle in Iceland. They farmed the land there and raised sheep, goats, cattle, and **poultry**. They also fished in the seas around the island.

One Viking who lived in Iceland was a man named Erik Thorvaldsson. He had bright-red hair and a long red beard. Because of his coloring, people called him Erik the Red.

Erik the Red married and had three sons. He had a special place in his heart for his son Leif. He respected Leif's skill as a sailor and shared his love for the sea.

Leif was the oldest of Erik's three sons. Following a Viking tradition, Leif did not grow up with his own family. When he was eight years old, he went to live with a man from Germany named Tyrkir. Erik the Red had captured Tyrkir and brought him to Iceland.

Tyrkir taught Leif how to read and write, as well as how to speak Celtic and Russian. He also learned to sail and use weapons. When he was not studying with Tyrkir, Leif and his friends would watch the ships come into the harbor.

*Leif Eriksson's father was Erik the Red, shown here in a print from 1688.*

About the year 985, when Leif was still a young boy, his father killed two men. Erik the Red had a temper and often got into trouble. As punishment for killing the men, the people decided to **banish** Erik from Iceland for three years. His family was allowed to stay on their farm, but Erik had to leave Iceland.

Erik said a sad farewell to his family. He made a promise to them. He said, "I will sail westward. Some men say there are islands out there. If so, I will surely find them. Then I will come back and get you."

Even though he was still a young boy, Leif wanted to go with his father. He told Erik the Red that he could help with the sails on the boat. Leif was not allowed to go because it was too dangerous. As he watched the boat sail away, Leif wondered if he would ever see his father again.

*The head of a Viking spear*

### Interesting Fact

▶ Leif Eriksson's mother built the first church in Greenland. The remains can be seen today in the town of Kagsiarsuk.

MANY PEOPLE ARE FASCINATED WITH TALES OF THE MIGHTY VIKINGS who lived more than 1,000 years ago. They lived in the northern European countries of Sweden, Denmark, and Norway. The time in history called the Viking Age lasted from about 793 to 1066.

Stories passed down for hundreds of years describe these men as "wild." They had no respect for property or for people. They destroyed towns and terrorized people.

Today, scientists have found and studied many places with Viking ruins. In Hvalsey, Greenland, you can visit the remains of a Viking church (right).

Recent discoveries have proven the Vikings to be very different from these stories. The Vikings were courageous and smart. They were excellent at sailing and discovery. They built up successful, busy towns. They set up trade between towns and between countries.

The Vikings built beautifully carved wooden ships. These ships took them farther than any other explorers of that time on the seas. The Vikings developed settlements in Greenland and in North America. They also founded the areas called Novgorod and Kiev in Russia. From the shores of their home country, they even reached Persia and China.

*Chapter* TWO

# *Exploring Greenland*

*When Erik the Red first came to Greenland, he found green fields. This picture shows Greenland's coast today.*

By 990, ERIK THE RED HAD BEEN AWAY FROM his family for more than three years. They were certain that he had died—that he would never return.

But, Erik the Red did return to Iceland. His people were very happy to see him. Erik told his family that he had found a new land. This new land had green fields, he said, and he wanted to take his family there.

Leif was pleased about leaving the farm. He loved the sea and was delighted

12

to sail to a new home. Erik called the land he had discovered Greenland. He gave it that pleasing name because he wanted people to settle there with him. Erik did not tell anyone that ice covered most of Greenland, though. He did not say that few trees grew there, or that the soil was rough and rocky!

*Erik the Red and his settlers set off for Greenland in 25 Viking ships such as this one.*

At that time, Iceland was becoming crowded. So several hundred Vikings agreed to go with Erik to Greenland. More than 25 ships left Iceland for Greenland. The seas were rough, and the ships were battered by severe storms. Only 14 ships reached Greenland safely. Erik's family, including Leif, had arrived at their new home.

*In a Denmark museum, this wooden Viking home is on display.*

To Leif, the new land was thrilling. He was proud of his father for leading the people there. The group built strong houses and other buildings near the seashore. The land near the shore was grassy and good for growing crops.

Because Erik was the leader of the group, his family had the largest house in the new village. The house was called Brattahlid, and it was big enough to hold many people. Some people settled nearby. Others sailed farther up the coast. The Vikings were the only people on Greenland. Their wooden ships were the only way off the island.

*The remains of Brattahlid, where Erik the Red lived with his family in Greenland*

The winters in Greenland were bitter and harsh. The people and their animals had to stay indoors to protect themselves from the cold weather. In summer, they tended their crops and grew hay for their animals.

*In Greenland, the Vikings hunted the walrus for its tusks.*

Leif and many other men sailed up the coast of Greenland. They hunted walrus, seals, and whales. The ivory **tusks** of walrus were valuable. They traded these tusks to merchants in Europe.

As Leif grew up, their colony on Greenland flourished. Leif had become quite a good sailor.

*A statue of
King Olaf
of Norway*

About the year 997, Erik the Red decided to send Leif back to Norway. Leif's ship, loaded with gifts for King Olaf, arrived safely in Norway.

King Olaf was pleased with the gifts. He also grew fond of Leif and made him become a **Christian**. Then King Olaf told Leif, "I want you to **preach** Christianity in Greenland. I can tell that you are a respected man. The people will listen to you and turn from the false old gods of war to the gentle Christ." Leif promised to follow the king's command.

*Viking mold for a Christian cross*

ERIK THORVALDSSON, OR ERIK THE RED, LIVED MORE THAN 1,000 years ago in northern Europe. No one knows for sure what year he was born. We do know that he was born in southern Norway. His name is sometimes spelled *Eirik* or *Eric* instead of *Erik*.

Erik the Red was one of the most famous Viking warriors. Fierce fighting between men was common when Erik was alive. As a young boy, Erik lived in Norway. However, he had to leave Norway with his father, Thorvald, because of his father's violent behavior. They moved to Iceland.

There, Erik married a wealthy woman named Thjodhild. They had three sons named Leif, Thorvald, and Thorstein. Like his father, Erik was known for violent rages (right). After killing two men, he was banished from Iceland. He decided to sail away, looking for a new land that had been discovered west of Iceland.

He called this new land Greenland. Many settlers wanted to come to Greenland to live. To build the new villages, Erik led a group of 25 ships loaded with people and animals. It was a difficult journey, and they lost 11 ships.

Erik was the leader of a village called Osterbydg. His home was near what is now the town of Julianehaab in Greenland.

## Chapter THREE

# A Voyage to Vinland

THE FOLLOWING YEAR, LEIF ERIKSSON AND HIS crew began the voyage back to Greenland. It was a hard trip with many storms. Leif's ship was bounced around in the powerful waves for many days.

*One of the best-preserved Viking ships can be seen at the Viking Ship Museum in Oslo, Norway. It was built about the year 850.*

When the winds calmed down, Leif did not recognize what he saw. He was looking at land he had never seen before! He realized that his ship had been blown far west of Greenland. He turned back east and headed toward Greenland. But he promised himself that he would return and explore the new land someday.

On the trip back to Greenland, Leif's ship rescued

several sailors who had lost their ship in a wreck. People thought it was lucky that Leif's ship found these sailors. The Vikings began calling him "Leif the Lucky" as a symbol of their great respect for him.

This 1893 painting shows Leif Eriksson discovering land in North America.

When Leif finally arrived in Greenland, he lived up to the promise he had made to King Olaf. He began preaching to the people of Greenland. Many of them became Christians.

The Viking colony on Greenland began to grow. More and more people had come to live there. The lack of trees in Greenland for building houses and ships became a problem.

Leif Eriksson and his crew probably sailed to Baffin Island just west of Greenland. This island is now part of Canada.

Leif knew that he had to find forests nearby. He remembered the islands he had seen on his voyage back from Norway. He decided to look for this land. With about 35 other men from the colony, Leif sailed off into the unknown.

The first land they discovered was probably Baffin Island. This island lay just west of Greenland. Unfortunately, Baffin Island also had very few trees and was very rocky. Leif named the land Helluland, meaning "Land of Rock Slabs." Leif and his ship continued south.

The next place Leif discovered was a piece of land covered with trees. It was probably the coast of Labrador. He called it Markland, meaning "Land of Woods." He was very pleased with this discovery but decided to sail on.

After sailing for about two days with a strong wind, Leif discovered another piece of land. He sailed the ship up river. Leif **anchored** the ship and went on shore to explore this new land. The ground was covered with many trees, green grass, and flowers. There were many large salmon swimming in the river and large deer footprints on the ground.

Grape vines were growing in the grassy meadows. Leif Eriksson called this land *Vinland*, meaning "Land of Vines and Meadows." He decided that he and his crew would spend the winter there.

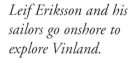

*Leif Eriksson and his sailors go onshore to explore Vinland.*

22

What is your last name? Is it the same as your mother or father's last name? In the United States, children often have the same last name as their father. For example, if a child's father is named John Smith or Isaac Goldberg, the child's last name will be Smith or

Goldberg. Last names are passed down through the generations that way.

Children in the Scandinavian countries of Norway, Sweden, and Denmark usually get their last names in this way, too. But it was not always this way. As you read this book, did you notice that the name of Leif Eriksson's father is Erik Thorvaldsson? So Leif does not have the same last name as his father!

Long ago, in Scandinavian countries, a child was given a first name at birth, such as Leif. The child's last name was the father's first name with *sson* added at the end of it. So, in Leif's case, because his father was named Erik, his name was Leif Eriksson.

Think about your own last name and the last names of people you know. Try to figure out which ones may have followed this Scandinavian tradition.

## Chapter Four

# Life after Vinland

MOST PEOPLE BELIEVE THAT LEIF ERIKSSON reached Vinland about the year 1000. This was about 500 years before Christopher Columbus is thought to have landed in America.

Of course, people still do not agree on exactly where Vinland was located. Some think Leif Eriksson landed on the coast of Labrador in Canada. Others think he landed on the island of Newfoundland, where Viking **ruins** have been found. Still others think he sailed as far south as New England in the United States. Some historians believe that Leif landed near Cape Cod, Massachusetts.

After spending the winter in Vinland, Leif and his crew went back to Greenland.

They wanted to tell the other Vikings about their discovery. When they got back to Greenland, however, Leif learned that his father, Erik the Red, had died. Leif was now the ruler of Greenland. He would never return to Vinland.

Leif's brother Thorvald decided that he would sail to Vinland. While Leif stayed in Greenland, Thorvald and his sailors began their voyage to Vinland.

For several months after arriving in Vinland, Thorvald explored the new land. During that exploration, Thorvald met a Native American tribe. He was killed by an Indian. His crew returned to Greenland and shared the sad news with Leif.

*This early map of Vinland is drawn according to old Scandinavian records.*

*Leif's brother Thorvald was killed by an Indian.*

*A portrait of Columbus*

For the next 12 years or so, many other people from Greenland came to explore Vinland. They even tried to set up a colony in the new land.

A captain named Thorfinn Karlsefni established a settlement in Vinland. He made friends with the Native Americans and traded with them, but the Native Americans soon became angry and unfriendly. Karlsefni and his crew soon had to leave the colony. Leif's half-sister, Freydis, also tried to start a colony on Vinland, but she was not successful.

Leif had a son named Thorkell whose mother lived on a different island. Thorkell later went to Greenland to live with his father.

Little more is known about Leif Eriksson or the Vikings in Vinland. The Greenland colony was thought to have lasted until the early 1400s. At that time, the weather changed on the island and it became bitterly cold. The Vikings then left Greenland.

*After Leif and Thorvald, many other Norwegian explorers came to explore Vinland.*

Storytellers keep the memories of Leif
Eriksson and the Vikings alive. These storytellers are quick to say that Leif Eriksson
landed in North America before Christopher
Columbus did. Leif Eriksson was a brave
adventurer who did much to help the Viking
people in Greenland.

*2000 B.C.* Ancestors of the Vikings move into Norway, Sweden, and Denmark.

*793* The Viking Age begins and lasts until 1066.

*870* Vikings from Norway begin living in Iceland.

*950?* Erik the Red is born in southern Norway.

*960?* Erik the Red and his father move to Iceland.

*980?* Leif Eriksson is born in Iceland.

*985* Leif's father, Erik the Red, kills two men and is banished from Iceland.

*990* Erik the Red and his family, including Leif Eriksson, sail to Greenland.

*997* Leif Eriksson sails to Norway, where he meets with King Olaf and becomes a Christian.

*998* Leif Eriksson sails back to Greenland and rescues a group of sailors on the way.

*1000?* Leif Eriksson and his men begin a voyage that takes them to Helluland, Markland, and Vinland. Erik the Red dies while Leif is on the voyage.

*1025?* Leif Eriksson dies.

*1100s* Christianity becomes the main religion in Scandinavia.

*1400s* The Vikings leave Greenland, perhaps because of changes in the weather.

*1492* Christopher Columbus lands in North America.

*1960s* Norwegian archaeologists find Viking ruins in Newfoundland that may be evidence of Eriksson and his explorers. Archaeologists also discover the remains of Brattahlid, where Erik the Red and his family lived in Greenland.

*1964* President Lyndon B. Johnson names October 9 Leif Eriksson Day, honoring the first European to set foot in North America.

**anchored (ANG-kurd)**
When a ship is anchored, its anchor—a heavy metal hook—is lowered into the water to keep the ship from moving. Leif Eriksson anchored his ship when he arrived at Markland.

**banish (BAN-ish)**
A person who is banished from a place is sent away and told not to return. Erik the Red was banished from Iceland for three years for killing two men.

**Christian (KRIS-chuhn)**
A Christian is a person who believes in Jesus Christ and follows his teachings. King Olaf of Norway ordered Leif Eriksson to become a Christian and preach that religion to the people of Greenland.

**poultry (POHL-tree)**
Poultry are birds raised on farms for their eggs and meat. Chicken, turkeys, geese, and ducks are poultry. Viking people in Iceland raised poultry.

**preach (PREECH)**
To preach is to teach people about religion. Leif Eriksson was converted to Christianity by King Olaf so he would travel to new lands and preach to the local people about Christianity.

**ruins (ROO-ins)**
Ruins are the remains of something after it has been destroyed or has been allowed to collapse. Viking ruins have been discovered in Newfoundland.

**tusks (TUHSKS)**
Tusks are the long, pointed teeth of some animals, including walruses and elephants. Leif Eriksson hunted walrus because their tusks were valuable.

**Vikings (VY-kings)**
Vikings were seafaring people from Scandinavia who invaded the coasts of Britain about 1,000 years ago. Leif Eriksson was a Viking explorer.

## *Web Sites*

Visit our homepage for lots of links about Leif Eriksson and the Vikings:
http://www.childsworld.com/links.html

*Note to Parents, Teachers, and Librarians:*
We routinely verify our Web links to make sure they're safe,
active sites—so encourage your readers to check them out!

## *Books*

Anne, Dr. Millard. *Eric the Red: The Vikings Sail the Atlantic.* Austin, Tex.:
Raintree/Steck-Vaughn, 1994.

Gallagher, Jim. *The Viking Explorers.* Broomall, Pa.: Chelsea House, 2000.

Humble, Richard. *Age of Leif Eriksson.* New York: Franklin Watts, 1989.

Margeson, Susan M. *Viking.* New York: Dorling Kindersley, 2000.

Simon, Charnan. *Leif Eriksson and the Vikings.* Chicago: Childrens Press, 1991.

Thompson, Ruth. *The Vikings.* Danbury, Conn.: Children's Press, 1998.

Trent, Lynda. *The Viking Longship.* Minneapolis: Lucent Books, 1999.

## *Places to Visit or Contact*

**The Mariners' Museum**
*To see an exhibit about the Vikings*
100 Museum Drive
Newport News, VA 23606
757-596-2222

**Smithsonian National Museum of Natural History**
*To find out about Viking ships*
10th Street and Constitution Avenue, N.W.
Washington, DC 20560
202-357-2700

# Index

GAYLORD